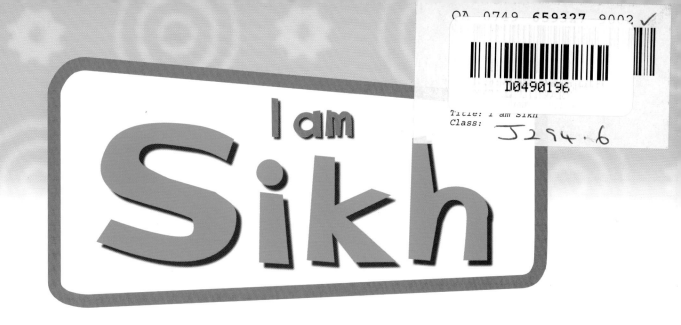

I am Sikh

Cath Senker
Photography by Jenny Matthews

FRANKLIN WATTS
LONDON • SYDNEY

First published in 2005
by Franklin Watts
96 Leonard Street
London
EC2A 4XD

Franklin Watts Australia
45-51 Huntley Street
Alexandria
NSW 2015

Acknowledgements
The author and publisher would like to thank the following for all their help
in the production of this book: Kulwinder Kaur Bahra and her students;
Jaspal Singh Sagoo, Naminder Kaur Sagoo, Jagjeet Singh Sagoo and Pardeep
Singh Sagoo; Kirpal Singh; Charan Kaur Sagoo, Gurpreet Kaur Sagoo,
Mandeep Kaur Sagoo, Hardeep Kaur Sagoo, Gurcharan Kaur Sagoo;
everyone at Guru Nanak Gurdwara, Sparkhill, Birmingham.

The photos on pages 12 (bottom) and 26 were kindly
provided by the Sagoo family.

Photographer Jenny Matthews
Designer Steve Prosser
Series editor Adrian Cole
Art Director Jonathan Hair
Consultant Rajinder Singh Panesar
Bradford Interfaith Centre

ISBN 0 7496 5932 7

A CIP catalogue record for this book is available from the British Library.

Contents

All about me

My name's Pardeep Singh Sagoo and I'm nine.
I live in Solihull, West Midlands.

At school I love maths and science. Outside school I play football, badminton, cricket and rounders.

I enjoy music and I'm learning to play the violin. In my free time I make electronic toys and play computer games.

My family

There are four of us in my family. My Dad, Jaspal Singh, is a research scientist. My Mum, Naminder Kaur, works in an office. My brother Jagjeet is 12.

Our names show we're **Sikhs**. Boys and men have **Singh** (lion) in their name, and girls and women have **Kaur** (princess).

Both my parents' families come from the Punjab in India, where the Sikh religion began.

All my grandparents live nearby. I often visit my Grandma, Charan Kaur Sagoo.

My Sikh beliefs

Sikhs believe that there is one God. All people are equal and were made by God. Sikhs respect other religions. They are all paths leading to God. We follow the teachings of the **Gurus**.

Dad and I are looking at a book about **Sikh** history.

The most important thing for Sikhs is to do good actions, and to pray to God.

Sikhs try to help their local community. I often give some of my pocket money to charity.

At bedtime I say prayers from our holy book.

Our clothes and hair

Because I am Sikh, I don't cut my hair. I tie it in a topknot called a jura and wear a turban.

We held a ceremony the first time that Jagjeet and I put on a turban.

When I'm older I'll take **amrit** and become a full member of the Sikh religion. Then I'll wear the Panj kakke or the 'Five Ks': Kangha (comb), Kara (steel bangle), Kesh (uncut hair), Kachera (shorts) and Kirpan (sword).

I'm proud to be a Sikh and to wear a turban.

Our food

Many Sikhs are vegetarian but others eat meat. Our family eats meat.

My favourite dish is my Mum's mattar paneer, made with peas and Indian cheese. Mum makes fantastic **samosas**, too.

(Left to right) mattar paneer, dhal (lentils with spices) and roti (bread).

The food at the **gurdwara**, our place of worship, is always vegetarian so that everyone can eat it.

I help to serve food in the gurdwara.

The gurdwara

On Sundays we often go to the gurdwara.

The Sikh flag, called the Nishan Sahib, flies outside the gurdwara.

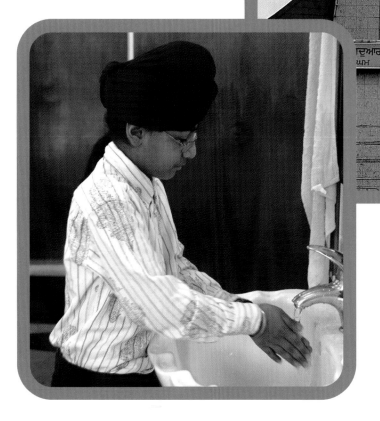

To show respect, we say a blessing, take off our shoes and wash our hands.

We bow in front of our holy book, the **Guru Granth Sahib**, and give some money.

We listen to the **granthi** saying prayers, and sing hymns to music. This is called kirtan.

Everyone takes some **karah parshad**, a sweet food that has been blessed.

The Guru Granth Sahib

The Guru Granth Sahib contains the words of the Sikh Gurus and Hindu and Muslim saints, written as hymns that can be set to music.

'This woman is reading a passage from the Guru Granth Sahib. It rests on a throne in the gurdwara.' Pardeep's Dad.

Our holy book tells us how to worship God and how to behave towards other people. We treat it like a living Guru, with great respect.

A fly whisk, called a chauri, is waved like a fan over the Guru Granth Sahib to show respect.

Langar

After prayers we share a meal called **langar**. Everyone is welcome, not just Sikhs.

People in the community take turns in the gurdwara kitchen cooking the food. They make vegetable curry with roti, salad and yoghurt.

Langar is special because everyone shares the same food. It shows that we are equal.

'Anyone in need, such as homeless and elderly people, may come to share langar at a gurdwara.' Pardeep's Mum.

The granthi

The granthi
leads worship in
the gurdwara.
He explains
the meaning
of the hymns
in the Guru
Granth Sahib.
When it is not
being read the
holy book is
covered with
a special cloth
called a
rumala.

Our granthi performs all the religious ceremonies in the gurdwara, such as blessing babies and marrying couples. He teaches us about the Sikh way of life.

The granthi gives me a rumala as a blessing.

Learning about being Sikh

Mum and Dad are bringing us up as Sikhs. We have a special place for worship at home. Mum and Dad help me to practise my prayers.

This is Guru Gobind Singh, who said that Sikhs should pray every day and help people in need.

On Wednesdays Jagjeet and I go to Punjabi class after school. We learn **Punjabi** so we can read the Guru Granth Sahib.

My brother plays **S**ikh music on the tabla (drums) with **G**urpreet **K**aur **S**agoo on the harmonium.

My favourite festival

My favourite festival is Vaisakhi, our New Year. At the gurdwara, a new Sikh flag is raised. Sikhs and non-Sikhs alike enjoy a festival of music, dancing, sports and langar.

Five Sikhs lead the procession from our gurdwara to the festival in a large park in Birmingham.

At Vaisakhi, my uncle invites five Sikhs to a meal. They stand for the Gurus, so by serving them we are really serving the Gurus.

Glossary

amrit The ceremony a person goes through when he or she is ready to commit to being Sikh.

chauri A fly whisk that is used for fanning the Guru Granth Sahib to show respect.

granthi The person who looks after the Guru Granth Sahib and leads worship in the gurdwara.

gurdwara The Sikh place of worship. The word means 'house of the Guru'.

Guru Granth Sahib The Sikh holy book. Sikhs see it as a living Guru to be followed.

Gurus The Sikhs' holy teachers. There were 10 human Gurus.

karah parshad A sweet food made from semolina, sugar and butter. It is blessed and shared out among the worshippers.

langar The dining hall at the gurdwara and the food that is served there.

Punjabi The language spoken in the Punjab, India where Sikhism comes from. The Guru Granth Sahib is in Gurmukhi, the written form of Punjabi.

rumala The piece of cloth used to cover the Guru Granth Sahib.

samosas Small, triangle-shaped pastries filled with vegetables or meat, and spices.

turban A long piece of cloth that Sikh males, and sometimes females, wrap around their head to cover their hair.

Websites

www.bbc.co.uk/religion/
religions/sikhism/intro.shtml
Information about Sikh history,
customs, beliefs, worship and
holy days.

http://atschool.eduweb.co.uk/
carolrb/sikhism/sikhism1.html
Information for primary school
children about Sikh history,
beliefs, ceremonies, the Guru
Granth Sahib, the gurdwara and
family life.

www.fairlands.herts.sch.uk/
gurdwaratour/start4.htm
All about the gurdwara, with
photos, and information about
the Guru Granth Sahib, the
Gurus and langar.

www.blewa.co.uk/project4/ch
ildren/C4_3_0.htm
The British Library special books
gallery, with information about
the Guru Granth Sahib and an
activity.

www.sikhnet.com/s/
SikhStories
A collection of 12 short Sikh
stories with pictures.

www.sikhs.org.uk/default.asp?
mnid=main&pgid=faq
Sikhs in England site with
common questions and answers
about Sikhism.

Note to parents and teachers
Every effort has been made by the Publishers to
ensure that these websites are suitable for
children; that they are of the highest educational
value, and that they contain no inappropriate or
offensive material. However, because of the
nature of the Internet, it is impossible to
guarantee that the contents of these sites will
not be altered. We strongly advise that Internet
access is supervised by a responsible adult.

Index